Sheet Music

By the same author:

Sheet Music

John Upton

PUNCHER & WATTMANN

First published in 2019
Published by Puncher and Wattmann
PO Box 279
Waratah NSW 2298

http://www.puncherandwattmann.com
puncherandwattmann@bigpond.com

NATIONAL
LIBRARY
OF AUSTRALIA

ISBN   9781925780420

Cover design by Miranda Douglas

Printed by Lightning Source International

This project has been assisted by the Australian Government through the Australia Council, its arts funding and advisory body.

Australian Government

Australia Council for the Arts

Contents

1 Words

Indomitable Irishry	13
The Book of Shakespeare	16
Macbeth Texts the Witches	18
Language	19
Leaching Calcium	20
City Daily Blues	21
The Liars	22

2 Love and Some Alternatives

Angel	25
Heritage	26
Sheet Music	27
Doorways	28
Greek Salad	30
On Sleeping with the One You Love	31
Pale Green	33
Tragic Thirty	34
Before the Flight	35
Eastern Daylight Saving Time	36
The Duchess of Malfi Never Stood a Chance	37
Questions You Don't Ask	38
Bellbird	40
Not Ending It	41
Three Months	42
January	43
Friends like These	44
Me and Multiple Bobby McGees	45

Summer Love   47
The Dance (Old Market Square, Warsaw)   48

3 Work

Another Day, Another Dollar   51
Heart of Glass   52
Salute to the Algorithm   53
Aquarium   54
Vampire Days   55
Living Doll   56
Michael York Fends for Himself   57
The Opposite of Us   58
Sex Was the Elephant   59

4 Rays and Needles

After the Nurse   63
Speed Dating   64
A Beach of One's Own   66
Orion's Constellation   67
Friend, Poet   71
Xander Kyle   72
Grief   73
Little Notes   74
The Poms Dance like Maidens   75
Survivor   76
Hidden   75

5 Time and Place

Visions of Old Leichhardt at Connie's Funeral 81

Big Time 83

Sydney Dreaming 84

Swamped 86

Salzburg 88

The Patriot 89

On Shoes Encountered in a Museum 90

The Larrikin History of Gallipoli 91

Crossing Galata, Istanbul 95

In Shrapnel Gully 96

The Hanging of Joe Byrne, 1880 98

Marienplatz in München 99

Peasant Wedding 100

The Conversion of Paul, Pieter Brueghel, 1567 102

6 Radiance

A Community of Bells 105

Agapanthus Dreaming 107

Diptych for Chekhov 108

    Connoisseurs 108

    Seagulls 109

Bad Agapanthus 110

An Intimate Act 111

Marvellous 112

A Visit from the Dead 113

Afterword 114

Acknowledgements 115

For my mother, Kathleen Upton (1917-1967)

1 Words

Indomitable Irishry

Gnarled Irish oak died peacefully. But peace
is complex. Peace, to Father Ryan,
meant inner tranquillity, not a surrender
to Protestant or Englishman. *Pax tecum*
was his Sunday. Then the Vatican
took his Latin Mass, and *Peace be with you*
was a foreign tongue. He understood
tolerance, and tolerated Rome
but had a special credo for some Italians.

In Cooma's granite country, cold and hard
as capitalist hearts in London (or,
God help us, Belfast), Father Ryan found his stone
church on a hill above the stoup of downtown.
Rotund and rubicund, *Irish as Paddy's pigs,*
(the congregation had its own respectful
disrespectful point of view), he sermonised,
his words dressed in their thick linguistic chasuble.
He liked to say things twice to drive them home.
'Your eternal soul will be eternally damned—
eternally damned! And you will be tormented
in the fires of hell ... the fires of hell! Forever
and ever!' He had a zest for it.

Sometimes I'm not here although I'm here—
sometimes I'm far away, sometimes so far
away the distance seems thin as this pane
of ice here in a ditch, a ditch not here, but one
in Limerick twelve thousand miles away
on some other morning of white-blindfold fog
reducing all to touch, sharp icy touch
as I lift this pane in Cooma, as I used to,

then a child but now a man, a lost man
who awaits the sun with certainty but shivers
until the sun of God will shine, firm up
this ague of home-sickness and dissolving
grey-white fuzziness, showing God's good purpose
to a sinner and a missionary outcast.

The Irish expeditionary force
flourished beyond the convict whiplash days,
it welcomed waves of exile and escape
from famine and the freedom struggle, Black and Tan
ran-tan with gun and boot and bayonet.
Out in Australia's colonies of faith
the seed was sown, the crop was grown, the English
were ravenous as ever—Holy Mother Church
required missionaries to guard the harvest.
And in the nineteen-thirties Father Ryan
took ship for New South Wales with its separate schools,
its Fish-on-Fridays, its watchful Tyke traditions,
trade union, Labor Party, anti-British.
And Father Ryan carried his Catholic Irishry
like a battle flag, proclaimed the Holy Name
and kept his brogue as thick as Irish stew.

It hurts, and they don't understand how much
it hurts on frozen Limerick-fingered mornings
a world away, in the fog of separation
from mother's honey-brogue, her love, her faith,
the kneeling nightly rosaries of family.
Sometimes I grind my knuckles on the hard
scaly trunks of pine trees in the churchyard
to punish myself for hurting, to hurt the hurt,
until the skin is cut and blood remains
on the tree bark, and I understand just slightly

how Our Lord Jesus hurt, the whip, the crown
of thorns, only the smallest, slightest taste of it.
And when I confess it to the bishop
he seems to understand, but then he tells me
gently that I must stop, that Jesus bore a cross,
and so must I.

His brogue a brand, his soutaned girth considerable,
he held his parish to its path, and changed it
by not changing. He found a separate sixties peace
in equanimity, standing profound
as Ireland's woodlands. His stoic sacrifice,
his exile and his loneliness touched Australia,
shaped its fibre, left it straight, and strange, and different.

The Book of Shakespeare

Traffic stretches and contracts at red and green,
late summer burns an epilogue on sandstone
and macadam as I cross. It's Shakespeare's birthday,
the State Library will exhibit its First Folio.
Tall storeys of antipodean glass
send courtiers into nuanced cool, and every face
becomes an arras, hiding an agenda.

The atmosphere approaching Shakespeare's Room
is reverential, almost mystical,
among this fist of worshippers—the word
made flesh and bone on stage, the lie made real
and bloody. We feel the lineage, we sense
the tug of tall ships through this secular
and sacred book back to a primal anchorage,
the forms and words now wired in the fence lines
and postholes of our thought. *Foul play, high time,*
fancy-free, stone cold, new-fangled, lie low,
in stitches, up in arms, and hundreds more.
A mall of archetypes and architectures
offers Desdemona's bedroom, Juliet's balcony,
Harry's Harfleur and Macbeth's witchy heath.

I ask the young librarian with surgical gloves
handling the linen-based pages, to find me *Hamlet.*
No page numbers, she checks the list of tragedies,
two openings and closings, and Hamlet is
telling the Players to speak trippingly;
I ask her, 'Turn back one page', and there it is,
To be or not to be, the words tattooed
on today's forearm, printed back four hundred years
and very near the author's hand, a hand

already dead, but now alive in Sydney.

I rearrange my mental furniture,
to find Macquarie Street aglow and rattling.
The ferry dips and skims its way to Manly,
where Arthur Phillip found the local people
impressive, with a well-developed culture,
as red-coat law-enforcers splashed ashore,
muskets loaded, Shakespeare in their shot.

Macbeth Texts the Witches

2moro n 2moro n 2moro
crps n this ptty pace
I can't do this. Since she stole Malcolm's mobile
she's been tweeting 10x a day.

IMHO, she writes, but In Her Humble Opinion
doesn't cut it with TMWG
because The Men With Guns simply text back
RTFM, and so you Read The Manual
but WTF, it says WCFY—
I'm Coming For You, too.

I have to try.

I lggd n2 yr wbsit
fr profesy bt al I fnd thr is
eye of newt and toe of frog,
wool of bat and tongue of dog
WTF?
Language is massacred. Lay on, Macduff,
and damned be him that first cries, *Hold, enough.*

Language

A tumble of tiles, a scrabbling on the table,
then the game continues. Letters are laid down,
words grown like cabbages in rows and squares,
an order civilised until it's shattered
and dumped into a box. A novelist
assembles tesserae of consciousness
into a speaking icon, with precise
dialogue that photographs the real.
But off the page and in the mouth, real dialogue
collapses in the kitchen and the yard.
Vocabulary's unhinged—phrases are ambulances
of maimed intention, coffins of evasion
and meaning's inferences are undone;
words harden to the fist, the kiss, the gun.

Leaching Calcium

The Herald tells me on page three
the caffeine that I'm quietly sipping
is leaching calcium from my bones—
no wonder their circulation's slipping.

I'm at a café table as
a woman in her twenties stares
at digits on her mobile phone.
Engrossed, enamoured, she prepares

to answer. Forty million years
of human evolution come
to their fulfilment as she moves
her talkative reversible thumb.

ROTFLMAO
can say I'm rolling on the floor
laughing my arse off, faster than
my poem can. But still I'm sure

what's imprecise leaves language spayed
and masks what's really being said:
'collateral damage' is the phrase
and not, 'the bodies of the dead'.

City Daily Blues

Men shouting 'Boy!' and plotting to impale
whichever women made the reporters' floor
rampaged through fifties newsrooms. Getting drunk
in bars, they missed the women capturing
the typewriters and swearing manfully.
Then newsrooms rode the sixties and the seventies
frenetically as bars became bisexual.
The internet arrived with citizen
reporters, labourers who'd work for nothing
but a credit line and narcissism. Classifieds
went digital and profits bled to dregs.
The news time-travelled seven hundred years,
redundancies advanced like the Black Death,
turning mental cities into villages
employing only skeletons. Now newspapers
are wastes of journalism, and a few old drunks
sit in parks watching the children play,
scaring parents by dreamily shouting, 'Boy!'

The Liars

Stabber Stevens is an advertising guru,
a salesman who can make a pair of discounts
seem like a clearance sale. And after work
he'll turn a glass of Tooheys in the front bar
of the Red Cow into a sexual orgy featuring
the Mayor and two secretaries. High-wire description
too outrageous to be true, but so inventive
you want it to be so, and half believe it.
As journalist and poet—man of facts
and man of buried truth—I listen, wondering
at his need to be believed, to keep the story
spinning (crying, moaning, now a click of handcuffs)
for another round of beers. How could he know all this?
Stabber leans a little closer. Because one of those
two secretaries is an intimate of his
whom he sometimes sees on naked Saturdays.
As he keeps inventing lies, the journalist
in me ponders the reputation of the Mayor
and Stabber's perverted psyche, while the poet
marvels and wants the colours to be true.
As an artist, Stabber understands that people
want lies, and want their hungers played upon.
He's a magician, not a poet, and prefers
lies that lie to lies that tell the truth.

2 Love
and Some
Alternatives

Angel

My father used to call my mother 'angel'
during the war, before the war between
them first broke out, before the fusillades,
the rain, the sodden jungle and the sudden
sunshine, the laughter, rage, the fists, the sullen
getting-on-with-it, before all that,
he wrote to her as 'angel' from his own war,
from the steamy, deadly jungle where he fought
thousands of airlift miles removed from her,
almost as far as later, often, when
they were very close. She kept his letters
in a metal box under their double bed,
she tied them up in bundles with pink ribbon,
perhaps by date, I never looked, being seven,
and embarrassed by this written nakedness
I found when she was shopping. I remember
seeing 'angel' rendered in his hand
and retreating under fire, too aware of
the hand-to-hand, the hand to face, her long-fused
burning rage at finding that her life,
being captured, was confined in this internment camp
of barbed wire and beer, his dull lack of ambition,
his rage against her rage, and children, children,
unbidden in faith and Catholic comfort, each
a map of love and duty, but a mouth to feed.
Having made that double bed, they lay in it,
and 'angel', having been written, never quite
flew away, hiding inside that tin box,
a hostage to their war, beneath that bed,
read by a boy who couldn't understand.

Heritage

My father hated Japanese—he fought
in The Islands. 'Little yellow bastards,
they'll never change.' He brought home malaria
and a samurai sword. In fevered sweat he'd babble
but he never said a word about the sword
or how he came to it. When he was drunk
and raging, my mother hid it; the sword became
a terrifying member of our family.

He's gone and I'm in Tokyo—pilgrimage
or accident. Sake and skyscrapers,
sashimi and a frost of cherry blossoms
in city parks, where friendly Japanese
offer directions. The samurai have vanished,
yet as I walk, the sword is everywhere.

Sheet Music

My mother used to kiss the clothes to find
if they were dry on winter afternoons
(us at the clothesline, me just eight or nine),
her lips more sensitive than fingers, sifting
the feel of damp from cold. She'd strip the sheets,
arms regular as scything, hand them, rumpled,
for me to bend down to the basket. Matching
each other's moves, we never had to speak.

Then back together to the living room,
cane basket handles in my hands. Inside,
an automatic dance, uncomplicated,
habitual—a bunched up, twisted sheet,
she'd smile and take one end and I the other,
we'd fold it first in half, then stretch it flat
and pull diagonally, left and right.
So routine, this. Our practised eyes would catch
and comfortably pass. Our fingers had
the right small pressure, never tugging corners
loose. We'd fold lengthways again, and stretch.
I'd raise my arms above my head, she'd step
towards me and the downward loop would always
miss the floor. She'd take my corners, brushing fingers
and I'd let go precisely. Now she'd tuck
the folded ends between her chest and chin,
adjust her hands, then let the fabric fall,
folding itself in half. Enough was all.

My mother used to kiss the clothes to find
if they were dry; years later, I still do it.
Among the sheets and towels, you search for things.

Doorways

Counting my blood, I click,
puncture a waiting finger
dialling triglycerides.

Blood is a ruby doorway,
my parents stripped of years,
my father with a cocky
slightly tongue-protruding
one-handed roll-your-own,
my mother at the copper
on Monday morning, heaving
with a wooden pot stick
sheets into concrete tubs.

In the doorway she's folded over,
her hands holding her body,
while my frightened father
runs next door to phone.
She murmured to him, 'I've lost it.'
On the bedsheets, blood.

The taxi stops. My mother
home from hospital.
Her open arms. The heart
leaping in the doorway
like my cross kelpie Rusty.

The solemn doctor gives
my father the complicated
verdict that's a sentence:
something called diabetes,
a swarming in the blood.

Through blood's doorway pass
my parents, singly, lost.
A shiver in the veins.

Squeezing a dark drop
onto a thin white strip
I test its heavy traffic.

Greek Salad

The supermarket chill-rack's newly packed
with fresh Greek salad as you and I, new lovers,
drift by, purchasing memories not yet
quite formed. The store is crowded but
our private space is full of easy aisles
for strolling arm-in-arm. Greek salad seems
perfect to pair with supermarket chicken
and crusty bread to share on my shaded patio
before we leave to catch the afternoon concert.
Afterwards, nibbling conversation's crumbs,
we find love has spread easily over everything
like olive oil from smudgy, busy fingers.

On Sleeping with the One You Love

You've found new love, you settle down to sleep;
it's easy, one would think. One would be wrong.

Your lover's back fits well for twenty minutes
into your spooning. Then your arm's the only thing
going to sleep—you turn onto your back

but can't spread out your limbs the way you do—
a cramped-up rite of sharing, of unlearning
yourself. Your partner senses this, rotates,

an elbow jabs your face. You both apologise
more than you should. You kiss. Your lover offers
a shoulder for your head. You have some doubts

but, as love's proffered, love should be accepted.
You tuck your head onto the docile shoulder. Now
your neck is crooked, you can't breathe. You both

stay patient and adjust. 'Goodnight.' 'Goodnight.'
You stretch out coffin-straight. When that's unbearable
you edge onto your side. The unfamiliar

mattress seems harder, lumpier than before.
The pair of you rotate like spitted chickens—
a rotisserie of love. And then you're under ...

You're half-awake again, the bathroom's calling.
Considerate of your lover, who seems to have
finally passed out—the breathing's regular—

you put it off. But no, your nagging bladder
won't let you sleep. You know that this disharmony
of bodies mocks your earlier gymnastics

and will pass. Not now, though. Gently, gently
you're easing out and down. The breathing changes. So
you whisper, 'Go back to sleep, I've got a big day

and really need the rest. I should go home.'
In your own bed, you fall asleep in moments.
Next day you talk, and love will find a way

or else, perhaps, things end as they begin.

Pale Green

Intimacy takes its forms from water,
immediate, adaptive, quietly flowing
from the moment—as when she pours the wine
and says I don't hydrate enough, I know
this proves she cares. So when she adds, my urine
must be quite dark, the comment comes from love.
I ask what colour it should be. Pale green, she says.
I check the merlot's nose (fruity and full,
as strong as Cleopatra's). An hour later,
when I report back casually, apropos
of nothing, the words, Pale green, she understands
instantly, surprised but comforted.
The colour is a topaz bond between us
and intimacy moves to other things.

Tragic Thirty

It made no sense, but perfect sense. As lovers
we'd revelled—theatre, concerts, galleries.
Now she screamed, 'Get out of the car! Get out!'
She was order, controlled, controlling, fashionable,
dressing up for theatre. I was orderly
but out of order, careless, dressing down
in jeans and two-or-three day clothes.
Love's magic seventy
and tragic thirty per cent.
Now, as she drove the car,
out of nothing, really, but everything,
she disdaining my opinion of the play we'd seen,
I objected to her tone, her character.
She hit the brakes then, screaming,
ordered me out. I looked at where we were:
down by the docks at midnight, lifeless streets,
a desolated landscape. Hours passed
in seconds. I stayed silent. Silently
she drove us to my car. We realised
this was the end. Alone and driving home
I knew, and knew she knew,
only two people still in love would fight like that.

Before the Flight

After the moods, the shouting, the uncertainty,
the breaking down, the breaking up—
the unexpected reconciliation.
You could be having breakfast here with me,
says the Mad Woman on the telephone
before my flight. The previous evening
I'd told her Mary and I had a deep
friendship, but still only of the mind.
I put my arms
around the lovely, mad, small frame, she folded in
to me and for a moment we were one.
I knew that what was right for that intense
moment wasn't right. I kissed her resting head
and slipped apart, I looked at her and said,
I want to explain to Mary that you and I
need time, but I need to do it face to face.
She nodded. Said she understood. This morning, though,
before I catch the flight, she needs to phone.

Eastern Daylight Saving Time

The day of lost time finds you making war on clocks
and never quite engaging as you seek
what you lost last night when she shook her head: 'You have
unreasonable expectations of what's possible.'
Now seems to be a past without a future.

You change the wall clock in the living room,
adjust a corner, walk back for perspective.
But what you thought was straight is out of line.
You go back close, adjust the hang, and try
to remember where the edge was yesterday.

Screaming noisy-miners near the window
flotilla-bomb a magpie as you kneel beside
the luminous face of midnight by the bed
where you perceived one future as she slipped
beneath the sheet in a language of moving cotton.

You press time-reset. Minutes tumble past
in weeks and months. Past last night's closing door.
Beneath your vertical clamped thumb, time streams.
Stops. Flicks forward. You stand as, in the distance,
a disappearing train is counting points.

The Duchess of Malfi Never Stood a Chance

The seagulls float like paper or walk in white
shirts and grey waistcoats on the esplanade
as she flies from her balcony twenty storeys up.
Birds promenade past tables on the quay
as she drops. Their feet and beaks, a red ensemble,
match her expensive shoes, the left of which
is now detaching.

Just an hour ago, she and her brother
sat at an outdoor table. As she stared
at her chocolate-stained cappuccino, he was saying,
'The Duchess of Malfi was staged in Shakespeare's theatre.
It seems that family problems never change.'
Using both hands, she raised her cup and sipped.
She grew a moustache, he brushed his lip and smiled.
She brushed her lip. Two seagulls were taking off
their waistcoats for a fight, or it might be sex,
they skittered and jumped. Sipping again, she wondered
why he'd invited her to this play, in which
two brothers killed their sister, who had taken
a lover, brought dishonour to the family.
Putting down her cup, afraid of certainty,
she said, 'You're looking sad.' 'I am,' he told her.

Red feet are dancing on the esplanade
then suddenly the seagulls leap and fly.

Questions You Don't Ask

She turns the page. Seems unaware
you're watching. In the picture window
lightning unzips
the humid summer night
and suddenly the jacaranda's vivid,
branches plunging upwards
like roots reversed. She looks but doesn't speak.
You need to be outside, you need to walk.

Infidelity corrodes, even if it hasn't happened.
How can you know? The sky's a playground.
In the street, edges shine
in the brief fist of light, and colour vanishes,
then thunder rumbles like a loaded cart. Your
body feels those needling vibrations.
Weekend conference,
three days away with her new boss. The night
is sweating and you walk soused in the everyday.
Past the railway station with commuters
scattering, thinking they can make it.
Past the beggar with the ragged cardboard sign
Bless you—don't judge. Past the taxi rank
empty of taxis, with its queue, and opposite
the full fried-chicken place where you used to eat
before she brought good food. Even at home,
home is always fifteen minutes away.

The air smells of rain. In the storm cell
blind energy is striding through a process
and you do have a place in it
but only as debris. That conference weekend
with her away, you ran into Maria
whom you hadn't seen for years. Went drinking.

The side street's quiet. Another flash—this
Federation house is down at heel,
a victim of its history. It seems
somehow to ask for one last cigarette
before the blindfold.
You walk on before the firing
and wait for the wet impact on your face.

Bellbird

A bellbird in the bedroom last weekend.
Strange in the suburbs. Dripping tap of tune:
two piping notes, one tone—first sweet, but soon
nagging, on-key but off. Melodious bedspring
or shoe-nail nightingale. It caught their blend
of beauty and bad faith, desperate for—something.

She'd heard it in the mountains, staying over
in the bush. She met her lover there.
At first they were together everywhere,
finished each other's sentences. Now she,
hearing the bird, is starting to discover
that where it is it isn't meant to be.

Not Ending It

You see the light, you navigate the wide
welcoming entrance to the dark complexity
of love in the lit carpark, you park beneath
the neon in the numbered space your husband
has given you, divorce is under way
as for you both it simply wasn't working,
and yet as you point and ping to lock the car
that same ping seems to catch your heart, aware
of love in a letting go that will be gathered up
again, you know it's hopeless, and perhaps
this is the last time,
but once again, for an hour, your heart
is feathery, you're a teenager, a bride,
walking the numbers on these doors, you're caught
in a love that lifts you up, you know
your landing wheels are permanently down now
but it doesn't matter, this hour perhaps will stretch
to two, it's an oasis from adjustment,
and if you cry at midnight they'll be earned tears
and somehow worth residual aching for
this sweetness, or so it seems right now as
you find the numbered door, you've seen
his car, he's in here, and you love him
as much as ever now the loss is definite,
and he needs you as much, just for this hour,
and then you'll come apart, adjust your clothes
and leave, your broken hearts relieved, committed
to the abyss, beyond an isolated
world of passion in a little room,
two lovers who each know the other's body
with certainty, without embarrassment.
You have the key, you're turning it.

Three Months

It was that sudden perfume. Things expand
beyond their own importance: a woman last
night in a coffee shop brushed briefly past
my unshared table—suddenly you were there
intensely. The woman knew she'd brushed me and
apologised, moved to the doorway where

she stopped and started joking with the waitress
about a man she'd dropped, and should she phone.
The waitress grinned, 'You have to make your own
decision, Jan.' She wiped a table, said,
'Do you love him?' Jan said, 'Naked on a mattress.'
'Keep him.' They laughed. 'I'll trade him in instead,'

said Jan and left. I opened my Camus
and tried to read. The waitress took my cup.
The perfume hung, I read four lines, gave up,
paid at the till, stood waiting at the lights
breathing pollution, too aware of you
and silences, and naked summer nights.

January

Sex-starved, shrill cicada noise
fills the trees as teenage boys
match cicadean desire,
fingers through the fencing wire

of baking tennis courts where hot
young women pepper shot for shot,
heavy serves and spinning kickers,
mini-skirts and matching knickers

show off scissor legs above
ballet-dancing feet that love
dashing cross-court, then a fine
needle-threading down the line.

Winners slumping to their knees,
shaking hands with referees;
from the losers through the fence
watchful wordless eloquence.

Friends Like These

Escaping into teenage ways
she locks her bedroom door, although
her mother knocks and calls; and so
the room becomes a universe
around a taunting screen that says
you slut you stupid moll and worse
for smiling at a boy they all
watched and wanted at the mall.

Embarrassing confessions made
to friends in secrecy are mocked
and trawled in public. Frightened, shocked,
she begs forgiveness, but the shrill
attacks go on. Depressed, betrayed,
she searches for her mother's pills.
With Facebook and a mobile phone
she thought she'd never be alone.

Me and Multiple Bobby McGees

Freedom's just another word for nothing left to lose.
—Kris Kristofferson

The Anarchist as an anniversary, dragging her
in his YouTube tow truck on a sunny morning
away from the washing to the Isle of Wight
in nineteen-seventy. The Anarchist loved this video,
a music riot as his fellow travellers
tried to burn the stage with Kris Kristofferson
and the band still on it, the music raw
as Bobby's ripped emotions, and her own
when The Anarchist moved out. She loved his hands,
his quick guitar hands that she gave the freedom
of the city, and the country, too. When leaving
he said not to touch his stuff, as he'd be back for it.
She got drunk and threw his guitar down the drive,
drove over it four times to get the beat right.

Her laundry's not the song's Kentucky coal mine
though it's waiting like a foreman. Now the YouTube
hook's in her brain. She's in Obama's White House,
Kristofferson, grey and grizzled, in a tux,
no red bandana, is doing it for the President,
and lined across the stage rock royalty,
a brontosaurus chorus, nothing left to gain
but weight and wealth. The meaning gone, they shout
the song and it becomes a coffin to her.
Someone's success is someone else's sell-out.
As she pegs her bras and knickers on the line
an aircraft scrolls the sky with *Marry me.*

The washing's dry, she can't forget the music.
She presses Waylon Jennings, gets the narrative
with fingering like the flying feet of Fred Astaire
and half the hurt left out. She clicks on Janis
for authenticity, remembering
a screamer, but instead she gets the words, the pain,
no screaming till the end, where it should be,
where nothing's left to lose. Janis awakens
the ache—like heroin addiction, love
never leaves you, it only goes to sleep.
She shuts down the computer. In the yard,
with the clothes on bar-lines and the pegs for notes,
she drops her single sheets into the basket.

Summer Love

Young lovers with too much time to bear
sprawl in the cemetery's shade
under a jacaranda. Heat
embeds itself in tombstones. Sweat
trickles, so they're not touching, splayed
and useless. Humid, sticky air
hints at a storm. They're purposeless,
oblivious of the address.

Though next to her, he flicks his phone,
speed-dials her number, 'Can you score?'
'No money.' 'Can you get some?' 'No.'
They disconnect. 'Or we could go
watch porn.' 'You've watched it all before,'
she says, 'And I'm too hot.' 'Alone
is useless.' 'Yes.' So, sex ignored,
they lie there terminally bored.

The Dance (Old Market Square, Warsaw)

Sex is on the prowl around the water pump:
eight sparrows—seven hens with quick, possessive
leaps attacking breadcrumbs, and the dancer,
the Master, prancing his obsessive
mazurka—his out-thrust beak grazing the ground,
he weaves and bobs and spins around, around.

He's puffing up his shape to show his size.
The females scurry, peck and dodge his dancing,
they're practical, attending to the day.
Rejection doesn't matter, he's romancing
himself as well as them in this old square.
Display is on the buildings everywhere.

He shows his potency below the pediments
that outlive death, beneath which youth, oblivious,
their guns all primed to fire, wander blindly.
Aware yet unaware of love's lascivious
immanence, they pass without a glance
the Master who bestrides them in his dance.

3 Work

Another Day, Another Dollar

Summer train, deodorant and onions,
forest fragrances, an edge of rot.
This is your day's rendition as you ride
the horizontal afternoon in peak hour's
meat-locker crush.

Hanging bodies sway in your parade
of weeks, as transit eyes flick off and on
like failing neons. In the seats, the stares
burrow for meaning or, at least, escape
in pads and cell-phones—

there is none. Time slows down into your station.
A carriage-wide, polite, ungainly wrestle
untangles bodies with a minimum
of touching. Now you're at the door, but know
you can't get off.

Heart of Glass

She loves her work, she is her work. For twenty years
she does it well, and then her manager
calls her in. The H.R. personnel
are there, they're never there. He says,
We're cutting costs.
She wishes in that disembodied way
she wasn't here in this high-viz environment,
glass walls, she wishes she was in
the toilets throwing up. The
world is glass, she's glass, blown and transparent,
breakable, but she's like those robots making cars,
as well, on auto. *There'll be a package.* She
signs the paper, she's at the hospital
when she had the miscarriage and grief moved in
like a lodger, and her husband couldn't cope.
You'll finish up this afternoon.
She goes to her desk and she's a box, a box
with a heavy hasp and a padlock through the eye,
a box of shards, of broken glass, the miniature
shattered toys of childhood—small and delicate
figurines, the cutting edges begging
for fingers, blood. Clearing her desk, she watches
from across the street, she watches through the walls.
H.R. say something, promising
references, three weeks retraining, at fifty-one
her best days are ahead. At home her husband
is living in his box, making his cars.

Salute to the Algorithm

Chekhov, Ibsen, Raymond Carver—
algorithms once again
tell their existential pain
rendered to a line of Java.

Algorithms drive your car,
run the rush hour traffic lights,
check the weather, cancel flights,
tell you where your children are.

They ask you what you want to be,
then, in working to seduce you,
they methodically reduce you
to Cleopatra's Antony.

Day and night the programs flicker.
Taking over government
they whip the Whips till they assent.
Robots have been heard to snicker.

Complexity won't let you drop them,
there's no option for divorce
when the fatal counter course
is turning off the grid to stop them.

Algorithmic rules embed
armed and elegantly fissile
programs in the guided missile—
no-one left to count the dead.

Aquarium

She recognises me and mocks my work
with her own lithe labour, arms like kisses on the
glass. Smooth as oil
she copies my mop and wringer, slipping her body through
a narrow ring of rubber,
eight handshakes but no hands and yet slim fingers slipping,
sloping elaborately—
she's a bag of brimming slosh and muscle, swimming.
Love was never like this. She
waits each day, we work, we talk, our conversation
is stately, exemplifying
her balletic, ropey, cephalopod undulations.
If alarmed
she writes her name in water. Food-grifter, shape-shifter,
she paces my walking
powered in the stroll by her three hearts.
My mopping done,
I pass on, she observes me to the aisle-end. Left alone,
she'll adjust her mantle
like a nun, then settle in a corner on a vigil,
a huddle of knots, in wait.

Vampire Days

Sixteen's the vampire age for kids
in summer cemeteries as heat
impales suburbia. These four
wait under a liquidambar, score
some weed then, wordless, sprawl and sweat.
Some coppers claim they're on the skids
but they just want to find a way
to bury boredom for the day.

They're shielded by the trees, from where
they watch the distant rectory
for warnings-off. The wife heads out,
they hide. The tall kid thinks about
her tied up in her factory
of prayer next door. He cuts her hair
in mental videos that recall
violent movies at the mall.

He scrambles up and starts to throw
a gravestone down, yells like the dumb
arse they call him. 'Don't do that,'
his girlfriend mutters. In a flat
frustrated tone that's full of numb
aggression, he's, 'I'm gone.' They go.
This vampire disease they've got
is being mostly dead but not.

Living Doll

Carnivore on carnivore
she primps as the media flash and cling
outside the charity dinner, sure
that cleavage conquers everything.
She understands photography
and daily editors. Her smile
is saying to the sisters, *See,*
most men were never weaned, and I'll

be honest, if you're honest, you
are bored and boring. These are great,
I started off a thirty-two
but here I am, a forty-eight.
Live by the knife, live with the stars
and help the odd good cause as well.
Your doctor friend can hide the scars.
A self-designing Jezebel

treading her own red carpet, she's
first in the limo, first in the lights,
and only barons get to squeeze
those beauties. As you watch tonight's
TV event, she's turning on
on coke while cruising off Cadiz
with millionaires. Until it's gone,
she knows that sex is all there is.

Michael York Fends for Himself

We're watching *Shangri-La* with the sound turned down
(Peter Finch and Michael York), and listening
to the cops at the door next door talking to Mary
after the robbery.

Mary was promised Shangri-La
in a remote cul-de-sac with friends
when she retired. The cops are telling her
there's a spike that coincides exactly
with school holidays (her mother's jewellery
has gone, and she's been cleaned right out
of portable electricals except
they left the vacuum cleaner).
Now as the cops are leaving
all notebooks and professional politeness
she cries and shuts the door.

Poor thing, you say, and go to comfort her. I sit
watching Michael York. I keep the sound
turned down. There's always this dichotomy,
the picture and the otherness, disaster
and the shock. Sometimes it's inside out,
like the Twin Towers falling in your living room—
the pictures are the truth and you're the fiction.

The Opposite of Us

Sculptor turning her to stone
giving her life
so he can die in peace.
She is his mirror, shows his self
to his inevitable madness
because his head's his enemy.

In Tirana, he says, *they won't let you build above*
thirty-five storeys because it's an earthquake zone.
He believes he's falling to pieces.

He pours in his desire and his need
she's his Medusa, turning him to marble
or salt from weeping.
In Albania, he says,
they shake their heads for Yes
and nod for No, the opposite of us.
The piece is finished. Chisel down. He bends
over the pond, he sees his face in water,
hates it. Destroys it with a rapid hand,
water is freedom, stone is absolute.
An earthquake's hiding somewhere very close.

Sex Was the Elephant

in the room at the TV seminar
on Turning Forty. Twenty-five invited
guests had answered candidly so far,
it seemed they felt important and excited

to be there. Then a woman said, being forty
and happily single, she liked younger men.
The female compere, clipboard and a naughty
smile, pressed her, *Why younger?* And again

that girls-together smile. The woman tossed
her shoulders, *They're better looking*, then a great
silence. The sexual hunger wasn't lost
on the woman as, caught, she watched them wait

as did we at home. She said, *Well, I'll come clean.*
The camera went in close. I surmised she
felt strongly that her private truth would mean
more, revealed on national TV—

the size of the occasion trapped her; so
she sacrificed herself, although aware
she'd wake up mortified next day and know
strangers had pawed her secrets; and yet there

seemed to be value in saying it—TV's
perverse like that. She gave her head a shake:
My last three partners have been Japanese.
The compere preened, feeling the elephant take
a giant step. *There's more after the break.*

4 Rays and Needles

After the Nurse

needles don't scare me but blood
well I never look
after the nurse puts the band on
my arm when she draws it I think
of her eyes or her accent she comes from
Iran or of all the phone calls
that I need to make I think also
transfusions are a great social
good but I can't bring myself
to ever donate blood about which
I'm guilty but fairly resolved
it seems blood is replacing religion
with doctors foretelling your destiny
even reprising your grandmother
which is all quite a leap from needles
and Shiraz in Iran she was born there
and the dark red dangerous syrup
rising that I glimpse as she's drawing
back and so I focus
on ayatollahs with nukes
and my huge damned car registration bill
which shouldn't help but it does

Speed Dating

People flung about the waiting room
by clocks, then tidied up into decorum
by silence and themselves. My own speed dating
was ten minutes ago, but still my name
keeps its own company.

I'm waiting for my call on the PA,
but a youngish woman watches me. 'John?' 'Yes.'
'Hi, I'm Mary.' We shake hands. Sit down.
Eye contact, quick rapport—this brisk but intimate
exchange will touch on sex obliquely.

Mary has the things she needs to know
on a quiz list. One by one, top down,
she ticks and crosses drugs and medications.
Your future's on the line, and all your answers
are correct, but you won't win the prize.

I'm waiting. The next woman, super-friendly,
younger than Mary, pumped-up smile. 'I'm Helga.'
'Hi Helga.' 'A few questions.' From a folder
she asks if I get up during the night?
Any spare parts or implants to declare?

Then she rises, leaves, still intimate
but subtly disengaged. You could be dying
and she's professionally attuned: 'It's nice
to have met you.' Rather than, 'Bye-bye.'
She's as smooth as ice cream and as likeable.

Sue beams and checks my diet. In a hospital
smiling counts. As Sue completes her scorecard
she tells me I'm in good shape. (Except for why
I'm here.) It's all about the radiology
and that machine they want to kiss me with.

A Beach of One's Own

More than a beachside suburb, she's your lover
for a nine-week affair. You have her number
on a card to ring if you're delayed,
but you never are. The hospital
has given names to its clutch of lethal paramours
like Darling Harbour, Opera House, Botanic Gardens,
Harbour Bridge. Of all the names, though, you prefer
Bondi Beach, a happy holiday
melange of sunshine, hope and carcinoma.

A kindly Genghis Khan designed the waves
that break on you, they utterly destroy
all that they touch. Each day at half-past one
you clock in, strip down to your underwear
put on a blue gown open at the front.
The nurses fit you carefully to a bed
within a steel parabola. A gun is aimed.
The nurses disappear behind lead sheets.
Gigantic sunburn penetrates your body.

Orion's Constellation

The platform bed
bumps gently like a train through points. The horseshoe
of the Linear Accelerator
is a giant new-fangled old-fashioned telephone dial
turning slowly and momentously around you
like Orion's constellation.
You lie in a magic circle
of deadly x-rays
waiting to be born. The therapists
withdraw to safety, Orion begins to circle.
It pauses, pours a jet of radiation
through your body
in a low-pitched aircraft whine. Your cells are dying.
The prostate, source of life, the source of death.
Twelve seconds and the zapping stops. Orion
turns again, then pauses. Radiant lances
the colour of outer space
burn within you—
life-giver and assassin
(eighteen seconds)
killing all the cells, not just the cancer,
asking the undiseased to recreate
themselves—you're told the cancer can't. Inanimate
machinery turns while animate machinery screams,
lights-and-sirens, bucket chains, the neighbourhood
rallies as a firestorm blasts through.
Orion pauses seven times. You are
mathematics, all geometry and angles.

When you ask if this same radiation ripped
through Hiroshima
the technician—he looks nineteen, but can't be—smiles

awkwardly to explain the technical:
'No, we make this with a huge electric current.'
This is your television set gone feral, turned
to violent marauder, its cathode gun
adjusted to Stinger missile. Photons sped up
to near the speed of light are surgically
directed. Doors, windows, ceiling
need shielding to prevent escape of scattered
radiation. The metal head of the machine
builds up toxicity. When it's turned off
it must be desensitised.

So science dispenses life, and resurrection is
a fact. Age backs away.
Confident as a priest
the doctor sits back in his surgery,
taps on his keyboard. He has mined your body.
'The biopsy shows your cancer has progressed.'
You've tracked it for a year like a wild animal
hunting in the dark, an appetite
consuming you.
'Active surveillance' is what the doctor called it.
For Orion has side effects,
impotence, maybe, scarring of bowel and bladder
can mean reduced control. 'Colostomy
is possible,' he warns you.
'But now perhaps it's time.'
Your choice.
And you choose science
for complicated, simple reasons—love,
loyalty and optimism; for robust
living in cruising summer before sinking
winter. 'One day,' the doctor says,
'people might even live to be two hundred.'

Would you want to live to be two hundred?
Gold Coast on the hoof, all happy hour
and cruising to Fiji and Vanuatu,
board shorts, golf carts, health checks, medications
until your cash or luck runs out—
then penury and petty crime
riots in over-populated cities
worldwide by the rising generations
squeezed out of work and housing,
while the wealthy few commute by helicopter
across Bass Strait to walled communities
in Launceston and Hobart.
Death
is displaced but cannot be discarded.
Those you love have gone there or will go,
and you can see the benefits, the ease
in ceasing. To be nothing, not to be here
in this sleeve of flesh,
to peel it off and let it drop
like a worn cardigan, to sigh and go
is not a dreadful thing if this same science
can end it peacefully and quickly. It is
not to be feared at 4 a.m., a step
into the dark of that unwaking morning.
Not to feel day clamber up the walls
can be a kindness. To go to what you were
before you were conceived, oblivious—
what's to be feared? Though
those who see a judgement
awaiting them from God must weigh the question.

A twittering like birds
tells you the team is coming back, ten minutes
is all it's taken. Tomorrow is

another day the same
for thirty-eight days, more or less, with public holidays.
Radiation answers its own question
on longevity, for it's a devil's bargain, someone says,
giving birth to other cancer later on.
The space within time is bought expensively.
Enjoy the out years.

Friend, Poet

It's sinking in. Inoperable
tumour in the brain. Not me,
thank Christ, someone I know. Suzanne.
Moved urgently to hospital
for radiation, chemo. Life
pinched into weeks, perhaps—a person
who lived by the brain will die by it.

Our bodies guard us, then betray us.
We trust them but they take to us
with knives. My mother had the knives—
breast cancer. Doctors cut it out.
The cancer waited for a year,
then quietly went back to work.
As I had, so I wasn't there.

This time there can't be knives. Suzanne
was healthy, full of time, and now
she isn't. Now, within a day,
the terminus is just one stop
away. The passengers are standing
at the door, and in the window
I see her eyes, they stare at me.

Xander Kyle

Born twenty-four weeks formed, in the humidicrib
you rally, start to blossom.
Then a crash.
Afterwards, the monitors telling us
your lungs, heart, brain seem to be functioning
correctly. But the doctors can't say whether
imperfections, stitches dropped, are being sewn
into your tiny life. Still, you survive.
Your father, this fully-formed future map of you,
creates a name, Xander Kyle,
affirming his belief.
Your mother drains her body, they take milk
to the hospital, watch through glass,
as you flourish on their love. The processes
of science—pumps and tubes and stainless steel—
mechanically sustain you while your body,
bequeathed by aeons, knits this slight, resilient,
independent life. Then crash—
your lungs collapse. The doctors read the dials
and close their faces.
After these sixteen weeks
your parents turn back time, must sign the form
and switching off their hearts
switch off your name.

Grief

The room
a humid black body bag.
You're prone for hours,
one voice
becomes a crowd. Then
thunder brawls,
needles through your newly planted
feet. Grief is a road
under a streetlight where
a cool spot on your face,
a dancing dapple,
firms into freefall.

Little Notes

These doctors—as she's older, it's never-ending,
breast checks, her diabetes specialist,
or the GP
wanting to switch her onto HRT.

She sits up late, revived by Jimmy Cagney,
Bette Davis and James Stewart on TV—
healthier times
before sick movies with their sicker crimes.

They knew life wasn't fair, but still they laughed,
got on with it. You knew that they made love,
but not on screen:
some things are better kept discreet, unseen,

including human bodies. And her own
is under siege. She keeps her private world,
but her daughters fear
something else is now becoming clear:

beyond her *tête-à-têtes* with James and Jimmy,
on the kitchen wall above the stove, handwritten
reminders indicate
new problems—and she's only fifty-eight.

The Poms Dance like Maidens

Australia is dying
at the MCG on Boxing Day,
five down for seventy.
He sits on the back verandah
among the fizzing kids and pool galoopings
big screen sound off
facing each ball on its merits.
He could have played for Australia
but for the demands
of family, faith and retail management—
Woolworths and Opus Dei.
Now he's forty-eight. The tremor in his hand is worsening
since the diagnosis.

From the Five Hundred game she watches him,
takes a trick, leads trumps, gets the seven
hearts she called.
Christmas is communion. 'Who dealt this rubbish?'
The daughters-in-law laugh.
She checks the time. Quietly he takes a capsule
as the Poms go up.
So does the umpire's finger—
the Poms dance like maidens.
He turns off the TV, angry, disgusted.
She watches him, misses nothing, angry too—
though never one
to dispute the umpire, she feels
God moves in mysterious ways.

Survivor

You're sitting in a mirror
in a wardrobe door
on the end of a double bed
mirror and bed both empty.
Full.
You wish this mood would shift.
The space behind the mirror is full
of clothes, all carefully hung,
blouses and skirts, all empty.

The bed in the mirror
is full of conversation,
some of it lewd, some of it loud,
some of it angry.
The mirror is a pond
full of flung stones.
You walk into the hall
the pond empties
while still remaining full and fit
for drowning in.

Hidden

Stretching up to look for a salad bowl,
I've found that you're a stranger.
Fifty-one red boxes of what killed you
bring you back instantly
months later. Why hide them?
I've no idea,
the blind geography
of long-term lovers. All I have left of you
is love and questions. And,
rage. I
take them down, tile after cardboard tile.
All empty. Why not throw them out? Why
stash all this empty air
for me to tumble in? And yet, another
part of me is grateful.
They give you back—
a secret you
I knew I knew, but didn't. That private you
who couldn't make decisions.
Calm,
I catch the red-stained packets in a bin,
I click the door-lock, step onto the terrace.
I flick your lighter
I burn these inoffensive, murderous
cartons, I burn them one by one, I burn them
like cigarettes,
chain-smoking emptiness.

5 Time and Place

Visions of Old Leichhardt at Connie's Funeral

Time burns your life like a stricken city, and memory
saves just the landmarks. Black and white, this photograph
stands like a stump or chimney of nineteen thirty-six,
the year Connie was married. The fire truck's polished,
the firemen uniformed and helmeted
like Prussian officers. Connie's brother is here,
machine-gunned by the Germans at Tobruk.

The bakery cart's one-horsepower between shafts,
canvas canopy, home-delivering
to streets depressed and shiny-wet with winter.
The baker was divorced and Connie, head stuffed
with wedding dress, chattered. He didn't speak.
Now he attends her funeral, speaks to me.

The ice-man stops to grin, lugging wet hessian sacks
block-cold, in his black leather apron.
The milkman's silver ladle talks to his cans,
ringing a rising octave. The backyard chook pen
is out of sequence, pungent chicken shit
and these six hens with rooster and cheeping tennis balls.

The two brothers are verandah-perched, their acrobat
fingers dark from roll-your-owns. They stare back,
Charlie blowing smoke and Bluey grinning,
eyes half closed. He wanted North Africa
with Charlie, but got Kokoda, and Kokoda got him
before tobacco could.

The dunny cart—Charlie and Bluey worked here, too.
After midnight, she'd hear disembodied voices
in the backyard, and darting footsteps stitching
the reeking outhouse to the truck in the lane.
Sometimes she'd wake to a sudden crash and swearing.

The album cuts me off. The century
snaps back. The family leaves the crematorium.
It's hot. Car windows are unwound, and nineteen thirty-six
is left to burn. The pictures will be lost
in a back-room bottom drawer. As I drive home
years wander back and forth. The city smoulders.

Big Time

Two magpies in the purple jacaranda—
shadows of their pterodactyl ancestry
they strut and hop, two officers, arms tucked
behind them, unaware they've lost a war.
Down here the war goes on, this tiny lizard
catching the garden sun was once as vast
as a dump truck, before the asteroid.
My kind was a skittering mouse, now I'm a fortified
tower and his kind is scattering
to dodge my sandals. Tiny creatures flicker
like torn nerve endings in the wounded leg
of Tyrannosaurus Rex. For Darwin, this
was evolution in its battle-gear
affirming the fierce divinity of change.

Sydney Dreaming

Renovate or detonate:
the newly-installed real estate
sign in the yard
of this California bungalow
from a century ago
shows what regard

the past has now. The greying grout
of verandah tiles is falling out—
some slip their casing.
With no repairs for forty years
the porch's balustrade appears
to need replacing.

Panels of stained glass art nouveau
within the windows used to show
the height of fashion.
Large families lived here and died,
were frustrated, or satisfied
by crimes of passion.

When asked about the architecture,
the agent answers with a lecture
on the available
shopping centres, buses, schools,
and how the public swimming pools
make it more saleable.

The short-term tenants are evicted,
the paperwork has been corrected.
The operation
is set for midday Saturday,
the auctioneer will clear the way
for detonation.

Swamped

Shrapnel eviscerates a sobbing soldier—
damp-eyed, I'm in two times at once, the Western Front
and mine. Then shrapnel-water drowns the past
as huge hailstones decapitate the cinema:
the flat roof buckles, tips
into the lobby. Filmed reality
becomes itself, what's gone, while we're the going
as we flee the trench and Flanders sodden fields.

Staff with wands of light are winding us
down fire stairs in the masonite and concrete
backblocks of their building, past black-snake cables,
into another time, a workers' street
from a century ago, where tiny terraces
are shoehorned one step from the road. I bounce
from year to year as carts and horses
become parked cars, and piles of hail turn slick,
inviting broken bones. With landmine footsteps
I approach my car to find it booby trapped—
this former creek bed
converted to an inner-city warren
by avarice and age—
has risen up, reverted, left my vehicle
flash-flooded. As I open the door, creek water
jumps out at me. Inside, the floor mats float,
the tray's a billabong.

If my 20th century electricals
won't rescue me, I'm stranded in a creek
pre-Captain Cook. The wipers heave their shoulders,
tossing crystal marbles onto the road
like trinkets from the 19th century bauble shops
in newly-fashionable down-market King Street. Now,
rescued from another century,
I have to turn my motorised paddle pool
into habitable transport. I pop the boot lid,
find a plastic bucket and start to bail
the baleful, unrepentant, timeless swamp.

Salzburg

Prince Archbishop Rudolf thanks
God for Salzburg and its salt,
and Beelzebub for Sophie Alt,
thinking of his lover's flanks.

In the mountains, under cope
and crucifix, archbishops scheme
to seize their neighbours' lands, and dream
of being Emperor or Pope.

Nuns in chapels chant their sad
entreaties for divine support
while, trapped in the archbishop's court,
Mozart feels he's going mad.

The Mozart-lover cleans his gun—
officer in the SS,
he's heard his mezzo wife confess
she's sleeping with von Karajan.

Hitler stayed here for the night.
Last year thirty-one per cent
in the poll for President
voted for the raging Right,

afraid of Muslims moving in
with five children to their one,
so they tell you. They've begun
to want the old days back again.

The Patriot

The claws are what distinguish her: beneath
the quiet delivery of dates and facts
is rapine. Lydia lectures to the tourists
in Krakow on betrayal that cries through
the bars of Chopin's music; how the flat lands
of grain were harvested in blood, and how
revenge is sweet. She taught at university
for twenty years until the Communists
discovered how she felt about the Russians
since Peter and before. She loves her grandkids,
her piano and clean underwear. She plays
the études with élan and passion, tries
to give up smoking twice a year, and guides
the buses. She tells you Poland had an empire
through half of northern Europe, till the Germans
and the Russians stole it all, and you can see
she hates them both impartially. If you
say to her the Nazis invaded Poland
she insists, 'No—Germans did it, they just say
it was the Nazis so they can pretend
that things are different now, except they're not.'
She insists the world is brainwashed, but that Poland
will rise again in time. Blood demands blood.

On Shoes Encountered in a Museum

The long black boots match the insignia
of double-lightning bolts at the man's throat
in this photograph, and the ambiguous
riding crop clasped tightly in his hand.
The knee-high boots are full of character
in their anonymity: marching to orders.
They're polished to a gleam you can't make out
in grainy black and white, but that's confirmed
by the wearer's wide-legged, aggressive stance
as bewildered people scramble from a train.

Another pair of shoes, these real, as red
as lipstick, wanting to be noticed.
Stylish, with cut-out toes, they take the eye
submerged by other pairs high as your chest
behind plate glass. The red stitching is fine,
the style impeccable. Shoes saved-for, you imagine,
weekend fashion for stepping out with friends
or her fiancé, after the week's black office brogues.
Shoes bought for better things than walking through
a gateway telling her *Arbeit macht frei.*

The Larrikin History of Gallipoli

a Brechtian comic opera

Roll up! The world's on fire! It's one night only
of massacre and mayhem over four
glorious years of sacrifice. And madness.
Oh, and Winston's plan to win the First World War.

Now, settle down! The Western Front's a blood-bath, right?
The East is cavalry in wind and snow,
and horses mired in freezing swamps. The south—
the south is sunshine. Winston's having no

luck with the Navy, so one night at the club
he captures Kitchener. 'We take the Turk—
we shell the Bosphorus and stick a sub
or two through Marmara, it's bound to work!'

Kitchener buys it. They'll put a screen of shells
around minesweepers and force the Dardanelles.

The big guns rock, the big guns roar,
the big guns rip from ship to shore
and shore to ship. The batteries
of Johnny Turk move where they please.

They shell our minesweepers, then change
position as we get their range.
So floating fields of mines still blow
holes in our hulls and sink our show.

It's very evident
to the Government
their batteries represent
a problem. Troops ashore
could wipe them out before
a final push, I'm sure.

So round one to the Turks! But all's not lost,
Australians are in Egypt, hot to trot
to Gaba Tepe. If they're shipped and shot
the colonies are keen to bear the cost!

Above the beaches Mustafa Kemal
is waiting with his German general.
The ships arrive at dawn, the tide comes in,
along the ridges, fireworks begin!

The Anzacs charge. The Turkish Seventy-Fifth
Regiment fights with bayonet—every man
is killed or wounded. The advance is halted.
Both sides dig in. They need another plan.

Johnny Turk, Johnny Turk,
you are good at your work,
as you shovel your trenches all covered in sweat
or scream up the gullies with fixed bayonet.

They told us in Cairo that you'd tie a rag
to the butt of your rifle to make up a flag
of surrender. But here on the heights you're just trying
to stick with your mates and get on with your dying.

The bodies rot
that graves forgot.
Maggots and flies,
crows in their eyes.

The Dardanelles turn into the Western Front!
How did this happen? Don't ask poor buggers huddling
for months in trenches. They fire, charge and fight
while generals check their maps and do their muddling.

A Turkish butler likes to hang
his washing on the wire.
He stands up slow and waves at us
and we all hold our fire.
This summer, flies and dysentery,
this winter, rats and drowning.
Last night a Pommy officer
got shot with his own Browning.

New German heavy guns
are hitting us. The Huns
have reinforced the Turk.
I fear it might not work.

Day by day in trenches,
you're so bored you can't sit still,
until the bugle's blowing
and there's more than time to kill.

Johnny Monash goes upstairs,
Winston resigns for half a sec.
In Cairo, their Lordships have affairs
while we all get it in The Nek.

The war gets worse. The Bulgars of Bulgaria
join Turkey. Now the British public's warier.
In Cabinet, the debates are getting hairier.
Keith Murdoch does a media splash that's scarier.
So Kitchener goes south to take a look
and recommends they should just close the book.

We've got quite good at subterfuge,
so when we have to go
we have some little stunts to keep
the casualties low.

Sea water dripped from pannikins
rigs rifles so they're firing
towards the Turkish trenches
while our boys are all retiring.

We make it onto troop ships
and believe we have a chance
to escape from hell a little.
Then they ship us off to France.

War's over! Winston and Kemal go on
to lead their countries now the fighting's done.
And in Australia, six rebellious States
with separate agendas on their plates
and mutual suspicions, in a national
government which is only semi-rational,
discover that in the barrel of a gun
blood and their Diggers' guts have made them one.

Crossing Galata, Istanbul

Flying fish
on Galata Bridge,
rods bowing and bobbing
like suppliants at a vizier's audience.
Each fisher has his own space program,
launch pad,
elbow room, bait bucket,
like this sleeve-tugging city. I'm
for the fish, somehow. Down there
there's piscine stitching of continents: Europe——Asia,
ferries and fish restaurants. Crossing
their sunshine
I pass between poles
of then and now,
a fish caught
in a rip of time, the zip of bait, the
howl of hook in mouth, it flips me
onto this bridge and off, too scrappy a catch,
victim of cheap jet fuel and wanderlust.

In Shrapnel Gully

Highway
a black military slash
through a corselet of Istanbul high rise
then elongated scrub
sprinting to Gallipoli.

Those other tourists
an accident of time.

Stepping off the transport
to grave markers lined up like regiments,
stunned by unlived age.
A market of flesh
in stone.

Beyond the fringe of beach
landform a starving animal,
tent-pole bones beneath a sunken hide,
gullies between gaunt ribs
where screaming men ran through its guts
with bayonets.

Suddenly
new soldiers running, amplified commands:

Clear the beach
everyone must leave the cemetery.

Brown's cows rush bewildered,
penned in Shrapnel Gully
near the car park,
sentences gesticulate to rumour,

Suicide bomber, explosions possible.

The waiting. The waiting.
For detonation, slaughter, body parts.

The Hanging of Joe Byrne, 1880

Human crows fly in to peck the body
of Joe Byrne, bushranger, himself in flight,
roped to the Benalla jailhouse door.
All of the crows wear hats. A fledgling, hanging back,
is still in short pants. They keep a wary
crow-distance, as though the body
might turn into a stone and fly at them.

Byrne's knees are buckled as though bullets just fired
are hitting him. He starts to fall forever.
But the dancing bushranger's been dead for hours,
shot in the groin, his femoral artery severed
when police trapped Kelly's party at Glenrowan.

He's not hung by the neck, as Ned will be,
but by his chest. The police have called photographers,
who nest around the body. One is draping
himself in black. The crow who took this picture
is further back, has opened his single eye.

Australia's first Press photograph
makes a statement to the world of crows.
And this is true:
a bearded crow in top-hat turns his back on Byrne,
he accepts, it seems, the choreography—
thinks that it's safe, disorder has been killed,
while murder's waiting patiently all around him.

Marienplatz in München

for Marilyn

Don't mention the war, or wonder who won it, as pairs
of very large *Damen und Herren* promenade
with very small dogs in this thirteenth century market,
for wars have come and gone, but they have stayed.

A Pekinese barks like a cough as it pitter-patters
with its mate around its master's polished shoes
and dodges a guillotine pram; hot tourists swarm;
time is ephemeral as the afternoon news.

The past has the present on a leash. The vulgar
recent eruption didn't happen. The plan
is to flaunt quietly Munich's sovereignty
and to erase the ranting Toothbrush Man.

The Old Town Hall, razed and rebuilt, is gleaming
in red and green, fresh as newly minted lucre—
the school of the Middle Ages points the way
without the need for Tiger tank or Stuka,

Munich knows that interest is compound—
interest on interest on interest. If you wait
you can be rich, although you're mad, or bad,
or a celibate priest who loves to fornicate.

The square is crowded, half the world converges.
On the corner, by a flower stall, a nicely
shone brogue stands waiting as a leash goes limp
and a dachshund sniffs, then lifts a leg precisely.

Peasant Wedding

In the dust and tar-strip roads of country towns
people think they know each other, so you're more alone.
The student with his sketches and his pencils
confides in his art teacher, who is married.
Her hand is on his shoulder as they study

the loneliness of Brueghel's *Peasant Wedding*
in another country town, in another country.
The first sitting's under way, but newer guests
keep crowding in. The bride is incidental,
sitting alone as background. In the foreground

a child scoffs bread, a man pours beer, two men,
knees bent, hoist a tray of poles and planks.
The teacher's fingers tighten as they recognise
the moment. See how, she tells the student, earnestness
displaces joy in all these people's faces.

She doesn't tell him it's as though the pain
of childbirth is already in the next room
delivering a hungry future. At sixteen,
he sees the bride, her husband missing, sat between
two older women, isolated, eyes closed.

Five hundred years removed, they understand
that pop-song promises can pass for courtship.
The bride might love the groom, but he's not there—
the town expected them to wed, so probably
he's outside roaring at the best man's jokes.

The young man feels he knows the scene, and why
the bride said *Yes*. Both Brueghel's sentry women

guarding her are tightly bound by custom,
two wheat stooks in a field. The bride is trapped:
this is how God intended it to be.

The Conversion of Paul, Pieter Brueghel, 1567

The man thrown from his horse disrupts the march
of Flemish soldiers struggling up from a ravine
to vanish into clouds top right.
The symbolism's clear enough,
life is a mountain to be climbed towards heaven—
but there's something else. This is how obsession nails you,
then turns upon itself. The giant saint is tiny
upon this godhead mountain, barely visible.
The horse upending him is Pride. Nearby,
a muttering knot of Brueghel's common men
unaware of history turning, 'Should we send
for the medics?' 'It's some kind of fit, I think.'
'He says he's blind.' 'We'll be late into camp tonight.'
'Back to base?' 'Not this stubborn prick. Let me help you, sir.'
A beam of lateral light is touching Paul,
telling the saint his attack on Christ has failed.
So here he lies, alone among armed men,
struck down by the mystery of his existence,
stripped of direction, stretching for another
while stranded on the mountain of himself.

6 Radiance

A Community of Bells

It's raining nuns in Croatia—
a fervent nation in an earthquake zone
of three deep faiths: Catholic, Muslim, Orthodox.
In a café on the Riva
in Split I finish coffee. Two nuns pass, laughing,
then half a dozen more, a sun-shower
of serene belief.
(It's rural poverty, says Emma, our guide.)

I was thirteen,
a student of Australian nuns, and did odd jobs
in convent grounds. The nuns were pledged
to poverty, chastity, obedience—I was in
the same condition. So I found myself
drawn into a powerful community
of faith that worked by bells—the day divided
by chiming into prayer. The angelus
was three strokes rung three times for *Pay attention,*
then twelve more tolled exactly at midday.
Sometimes I'd get to ring them, and would eavesdrop
on the whisper of robes and hurry of shoes to worship.
The plaited hymns I heard from the chapel window
changed by season, tinged with the happiness
of fasting and denial. All these women
wore long black tunics, knew my name, and smiled
at me differently from the yelling schoolyard boys.
Among nuns I was part of a communion,
one of the chosen,
even when raking chook shit from the hen house.

On the Riva, another gust of nuns.
The bells of angelus tolled here for war

as teenage boys with shining eyes and hymns
in their throats took up their weapons, and died,
throats cut, blood shed for Christ. I wait
beside our bus as the nuns pass, fervent, lovely,
full of that certainty I've lost. I wish them well.
Bosnia is waiting.

Agapanthus Dreaming

Australian summer on stilts, the agapanthus keep coming,
a festival of tall, they're a high-rise, high-wire
dancing answer to tiny gardens, a vertical shout,
they're cliff-top parties in mauve and white dresses, they're
clean-stalked, green-stalked teens surfing the wind,
sliding its breakers, breaking bomboras. Their ring-top flowers
are choirs of hallelujah to heat and sun, they're
wild white coronas, colour-collars, December's dreadlocks,
floral migraines, they're visible Satchmo solos trumpet-clustered.

In cicada-trilled, friends-over afternoons on festive patios
they're a swaying, laughing, bon-moting tilting of champagne flutes,
they're towers of frozen jazz, a Broadway for bees
and their bulging knees in the heat, a chorus line
of slender legs, they're Tiffany explosions of stopped light,
burst bubbles of tonic frozen. Calm in the laughter,
they're slim as a supermodel, they say, 'Hold my drink—
take my photograph!'

Wild as the Mad Professor in movie matinees,
they're a hectic windy chase of pistil-whipped petals
folding out female welcome. Fertile as Jurassic
jungle, they're rifled treasure, lost arks of nectar,
fire escapes for bugs from towering heat. In rain
they're crowns of glistening worry, thrones of water
bowed dangerously with gravity. But in sun again
they're Isadora—swaying, a shock of umbels
ringing colour. They're a bewildered sadness, 'I'm
so lovely—why won't I live forever?'

Diptych for Chekhov

Connoisseurs

Anton Chekhov was a connoisseur of brothels,
says the lecturer, then the flocked seagulls scatter
and form a disorderly tea-urn queue. Briony thinks
the lecturer's naïve, so what should Chekhov do,
unwed at forty, rich, just tie a knot in it?
Get some ingénue in trouble, wreck a marriage?
She hasn't shared with him that she's played Nina
twice, had her heart broken by her leading man
and would be Chekhov's lover in an instant,
(provided he wasn't reeking of tobacco).
He understood the solitary life
has dangers, it drove Nietzsche mad. Briony
has learned she must protect herself. Like Chekhov
characters, each knows the other's watching.
She approaches, he flicks the book of plays; he needs
more than her friendship, she wants less than love.

Seagulls

Anton Chekhov was a connoisseur of brothels—
you hear unusual things at U3A,
the Soviet archives have been coughing up
real blood, says Helen over morning coffee as
the women come and go talking of—no,
that was another week. Christina says
over the snappy chatter that Chekhov did
eventually get married at forty-one,
she read it on the internet, his leading
lady, but far too late, within three years
he died, it's all on Wikipedia. Kevin says,
Tuberculosis killed him, it's amazing,
he kept denying it, he must have known,
he was a doctor. Ruth adds, Died in Germany,
they shipped him back to Moscow chilled inside
a refrigerated train car of fresh oysters,
he was an oyster connoisseur, adored them.
Mary's thinking, Chekhov would have loved
that story; but all the chatter and ephemera
utterly lose the largeness of a man.

Bad Agapanthus

Ask a farmer: he'll tell you a Raymond Chandler blonde
is less dangerous, less likely to spread risky rhizomes
than these charmers with rocket legs, with cigarette holders
as long as your arm, who'll strangle you in your sleep
and steal your paddocks, calling the long goodbye.

He sees through their stockinged elegance, their colour,
their presence in ones or twos. He understands
how a single caravan on a neighbouring property
can lead to a bikie stockade with drugs and shotguns.

He knows how agapanthus creeps quietly through towns
then thickens and sprouts. It bolts on a slosh of wind
spreading its seed like a convoy of rock'n'roll roadies.
The next generation stampedes like music fans,
it explodes like teenage music, taking over the world.

An Intimate Act

'A tiny sting,' she says, and slips the needle
into the blue factory
of my inner elbow, introducing me
to my life force. Her face near mine, she's
drawing the red nectar. She's gentle, slow. I
feel a little faint and look away.
The dark melange of hope and lust and sadness
goes into tiny flowerpots, smoothly, smoothly,
to grow its essence and be analysed.
She's intent. Inside my head
my cast of characters is chattering,
most hating blood. Her hands are full of knowledge.
'Can you hold this?'
I press the cotton wool down on the wound,
she adds a sticking plaster. I tug my sleeve,
we draw apart,
put on our personalities.
As I prepare
to face the rushing gutters of the rain
she's in the doorway. Passing her, I know
I could adore her in another life.

Marvellous

Ugly midget butler, frock-coat brown
and crisp, without a wrinkle. Antennae
diligent and quick as any butler's
eyebrows. I catch it waiting on the cat's food
and fold its cockroach legs under my shoe.
The lifted foot shows water that's not water
but magical nucleic acid powering
the delicate and marvellous machinery
that's driven it for eons, time far longer
than mine, its foot soldier. Where I'd die foaming,
it can dine on rat poison and flourish
(some lawyers come to mind). Its feelers take it
through the argument of darkness in a cupboard
where I'd be helpless, terrified. It has
more nationalities than we do, and could speak
German in Kafka's day. It usually
could dance zigzagging around my two left feet.
All that complexity. I wipe it with a tissue.

A Visit from the Dead

A visit from the dead should be profound,
never domestic. But my wife was practical.
Last night she half-filled the electric jug,
turned it on,
set out our usual two mugs for tea.
She was wearing her blue nightdress with the pink bows
across the bodice. I said to her,
'You're dead.' She simply poured the tea, 'I'm not.'
I was definite, 'You are.' We calmly disagreed
as we did sometimes over, say, who hadn't
put milk back in the fridge, or hadn't made
a phone call. Then she said, 'How are you?'
I said, 'You're not aware?' 'Yes, I'm aware.'
We let it go, as married couples do.
I said, 'Tea's nice. But I've moved on to tea bags.'
She said, 'You don't play music anymore.'
'Music is dangerous.' 'That's sad.' 'It is.'
'I've discovered Dante loves orchestral.'
'Which composers? Those post-Dante? Beethoven?'
'I'm not allowed to tell you.' We drank tea,
discussed Dante and Beatrice a little,
but what she said escapes me. I can't say
how or when she left again, but when I woke
knowing it wasn't true, I knew it was.

Afterword

In 2017, a week before his untimely death, John Upton entrusted Margaret Bradstock and Louise Wakeling with manuscript copies of his latest poetry collection, for comment and suggestion. After consultation with the executor of John's estate they have, together with colleague Gisela Nittel, edited the manuscript for publication. The title, *Sheet Music* (from the poem of the same name), was suggested by Julie Nebauer, John's sister-in-law and executor, and is an apt descriptor for this book. For those who knew and valued John's friendship and support, this final collection will be a welcome addition to his *oeuvre*, and a testament to his significant contribution as a poet.

Acknowledgements

Poems in this collection have appeared in the following publications:

Australian Poetry Anthology (2016), *Australian Poetry Journal* (6.1), *Award Winning Australian Writing* (2015), *Cordite, Overland, Peace, tolerance and understanding: poems from the ACU 2015 prize for poetry, Plumwood Mountain, Quadrant, The Australian, The Best Australian Poems* (2015 and 2017), *Transnational Literature* (May, 2015).

www.ingramcontent.com/pod-product-compliance
Lightning Source LLC
Chambersburg PA
CBHW030846090426
42737CB00009B/1121